What is Fun?

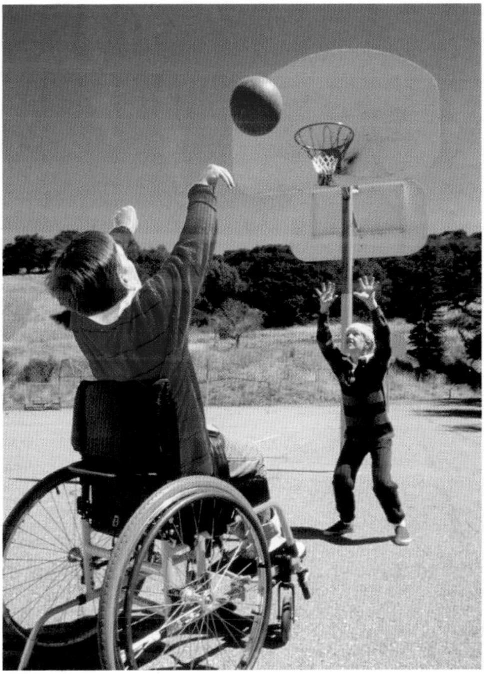

written by Pam Holden

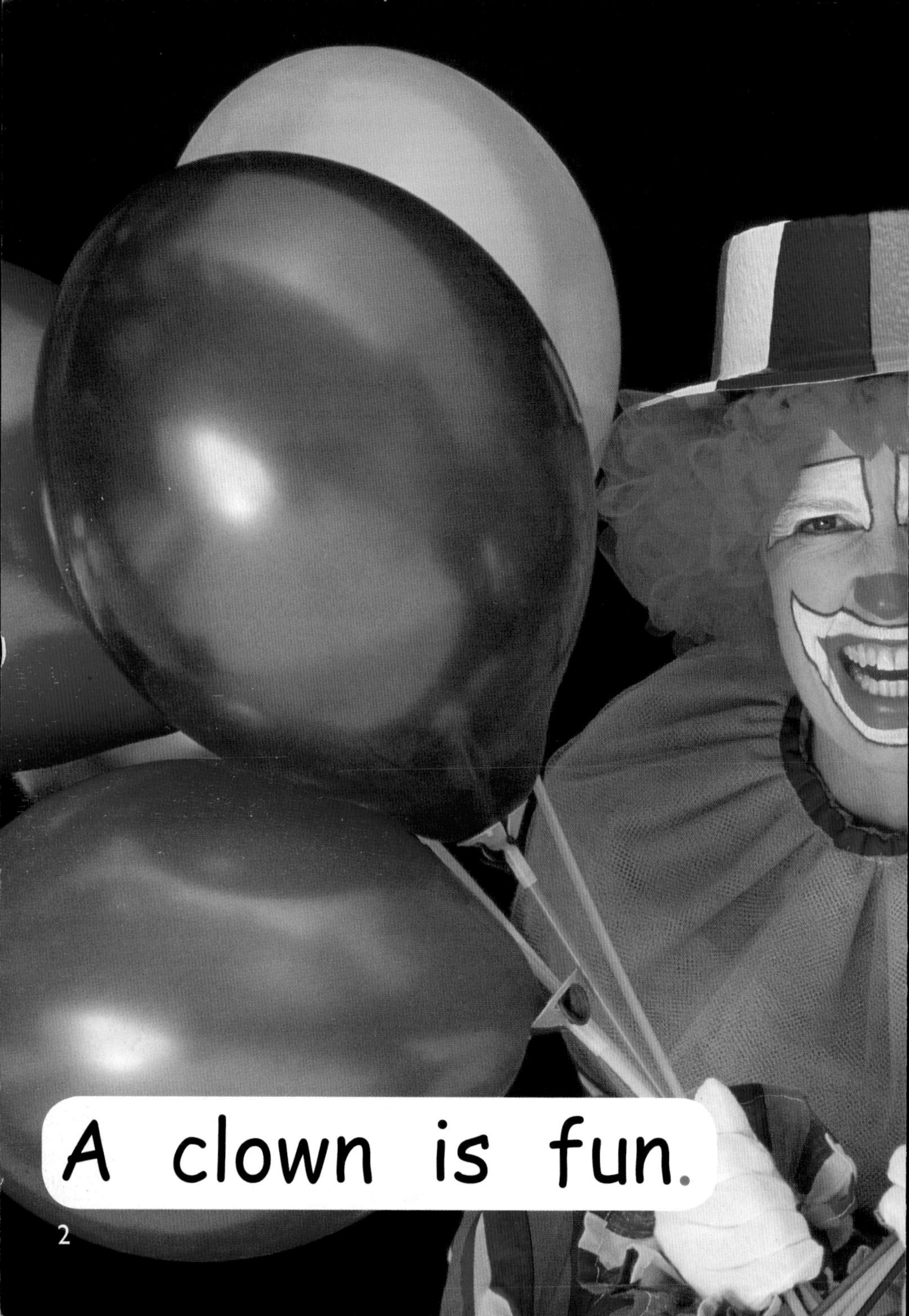

A clown is fun.

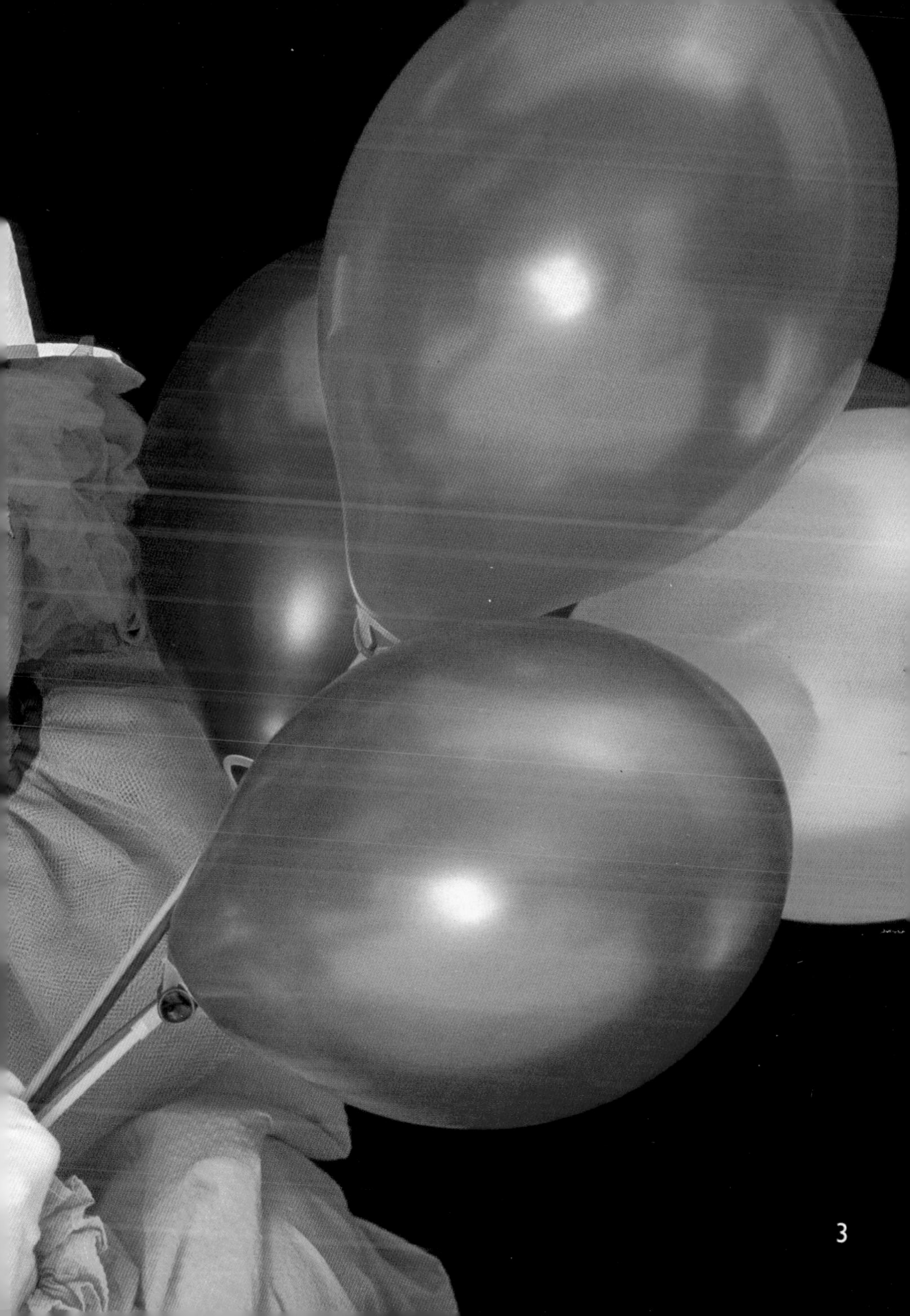

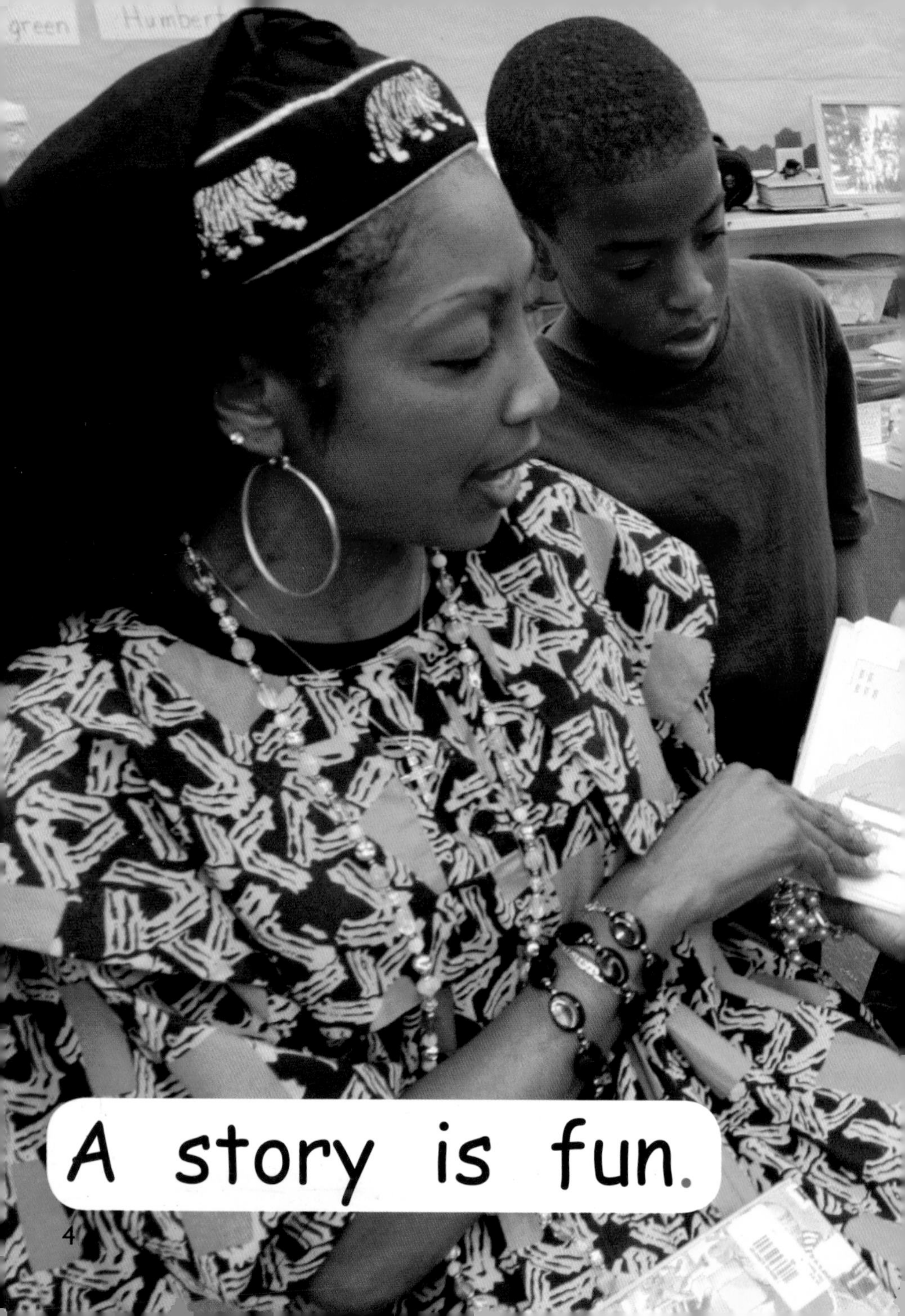

A story is fun.

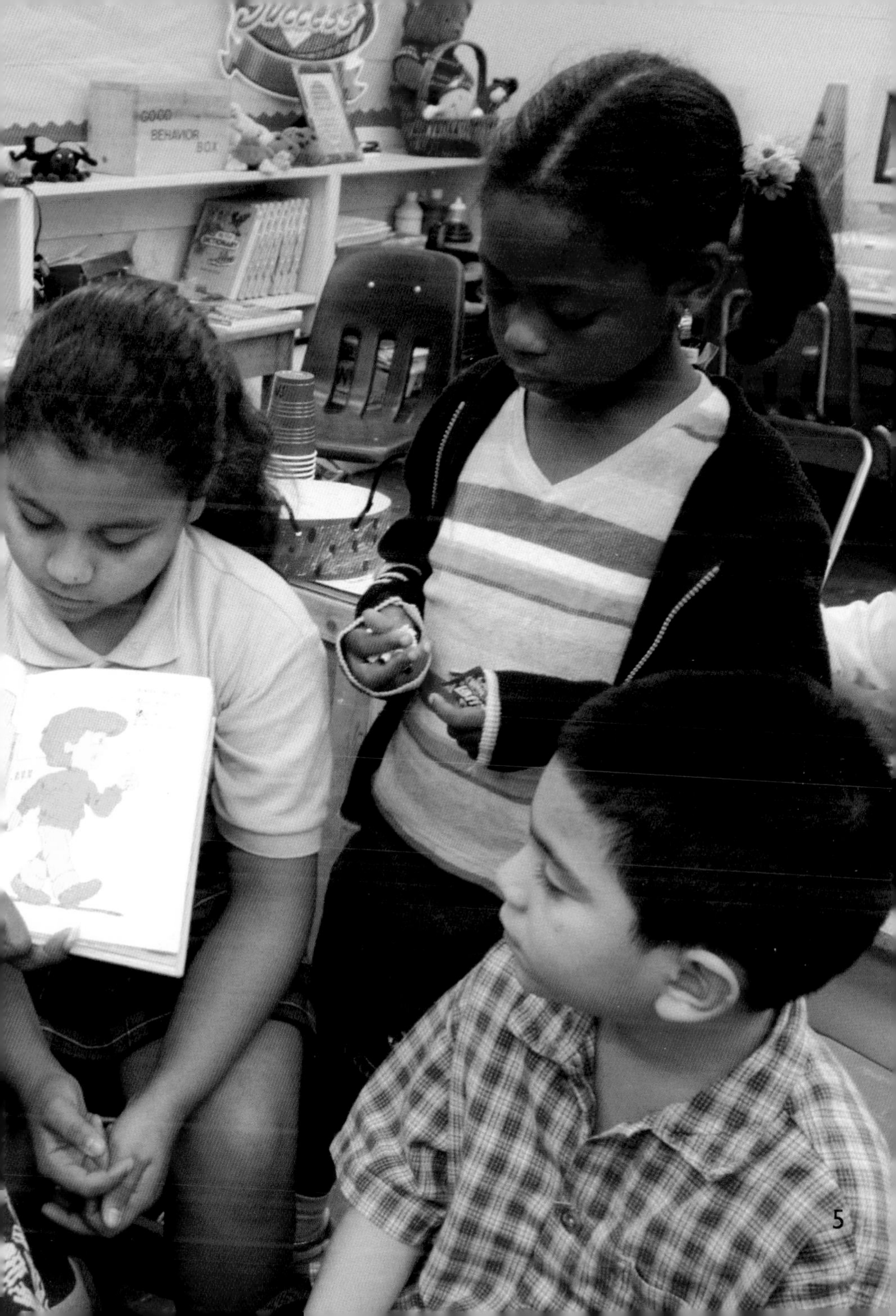
GOOD
BEHAVIOR
BOX

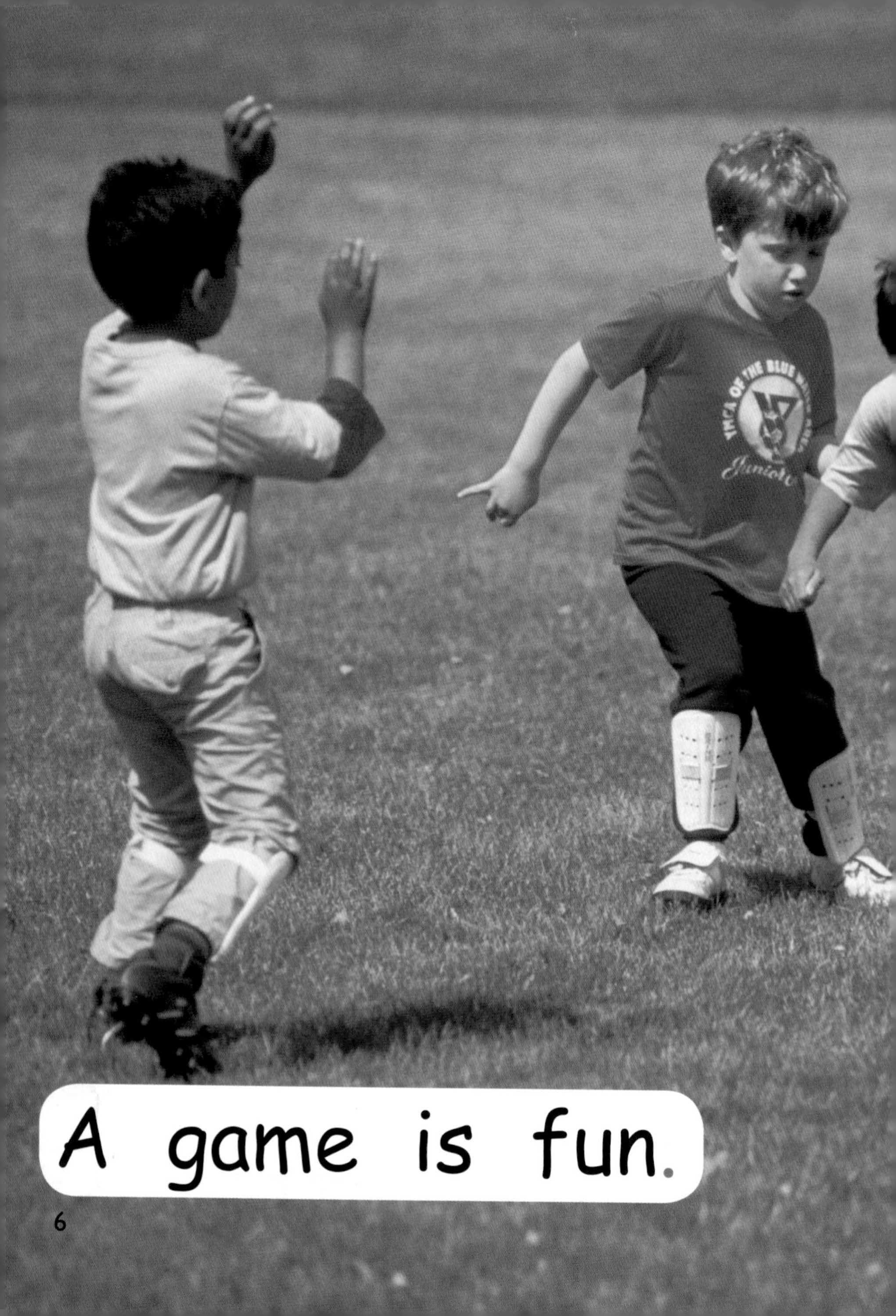

A game is fun.

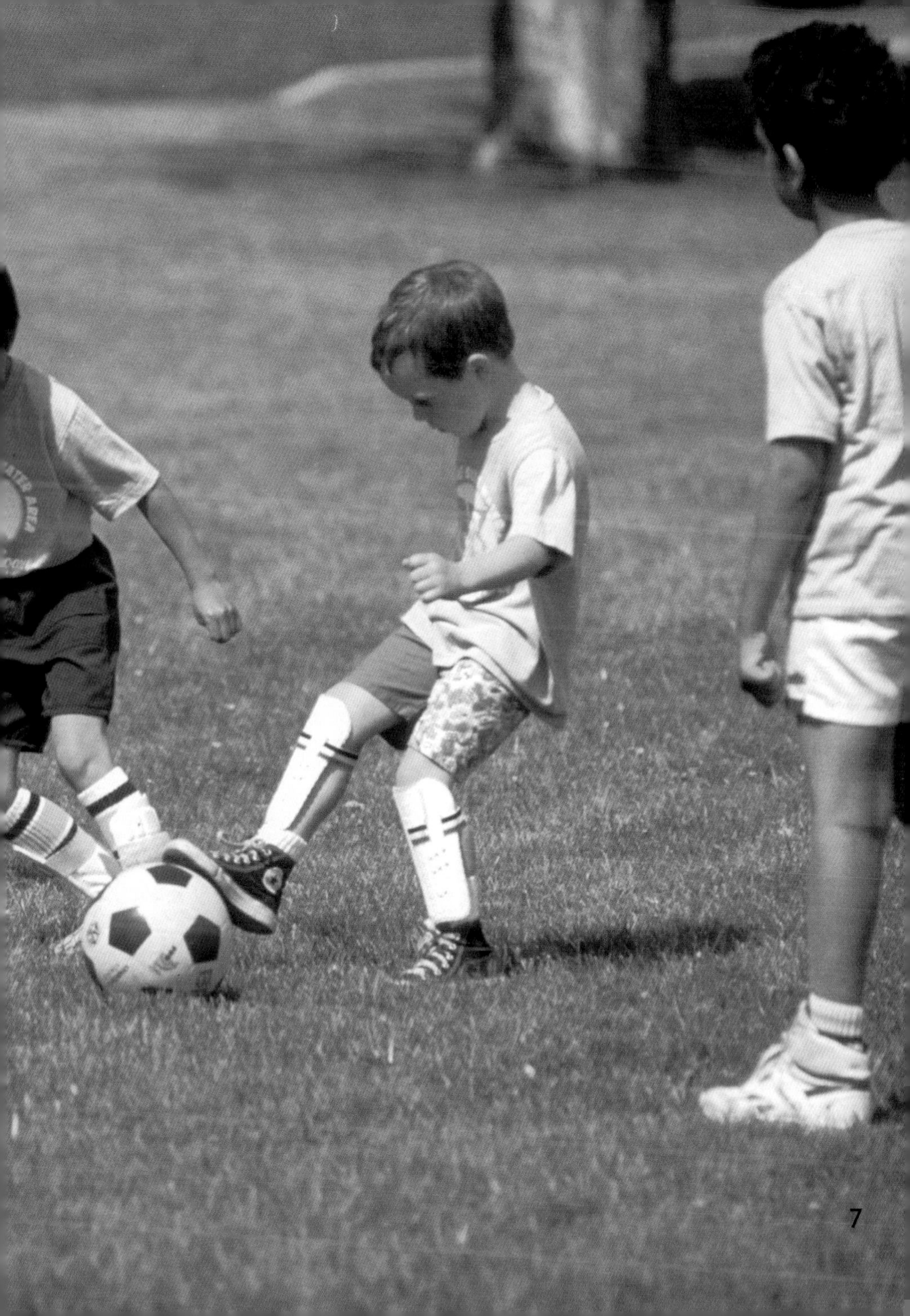

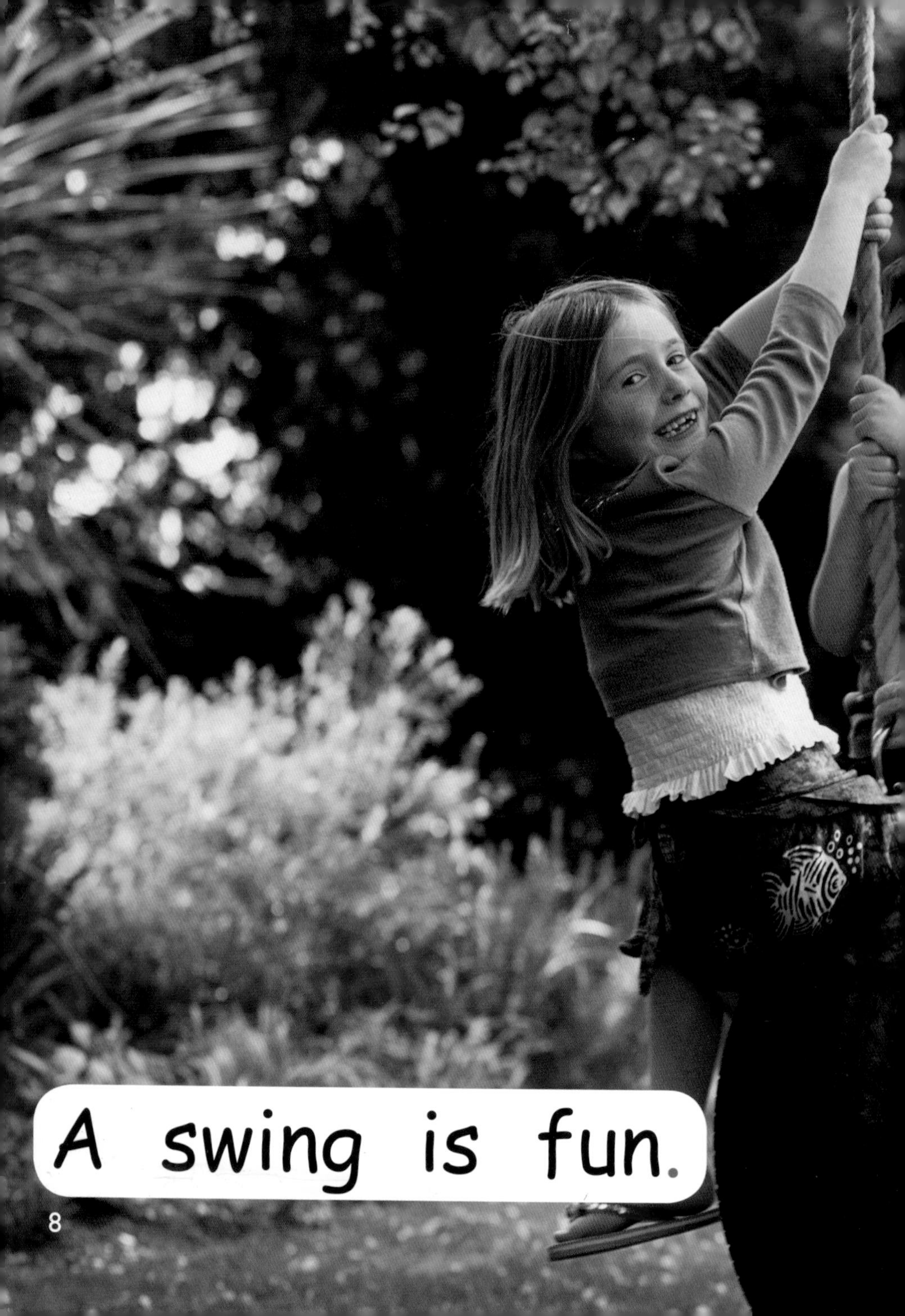

A swing is fun.

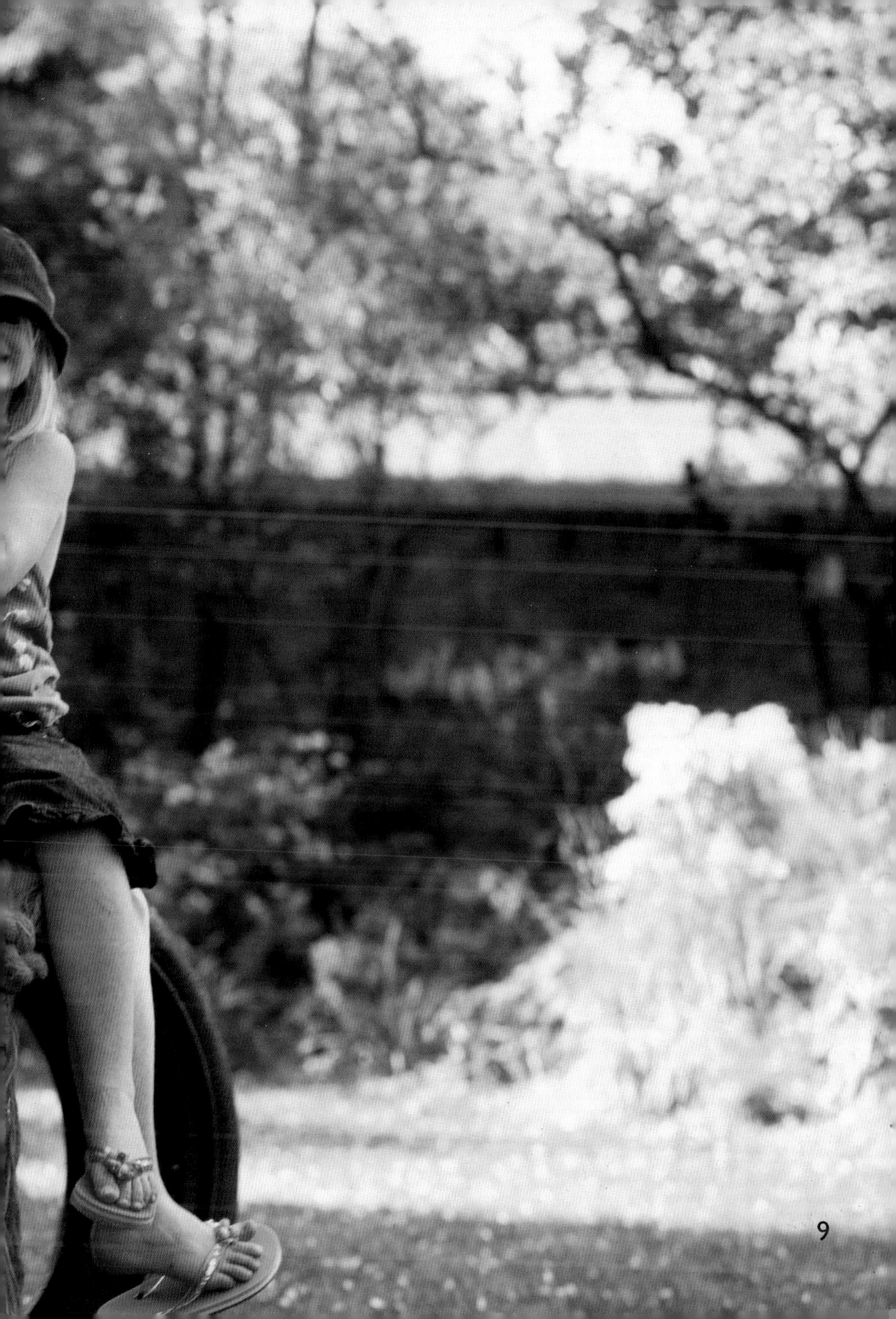

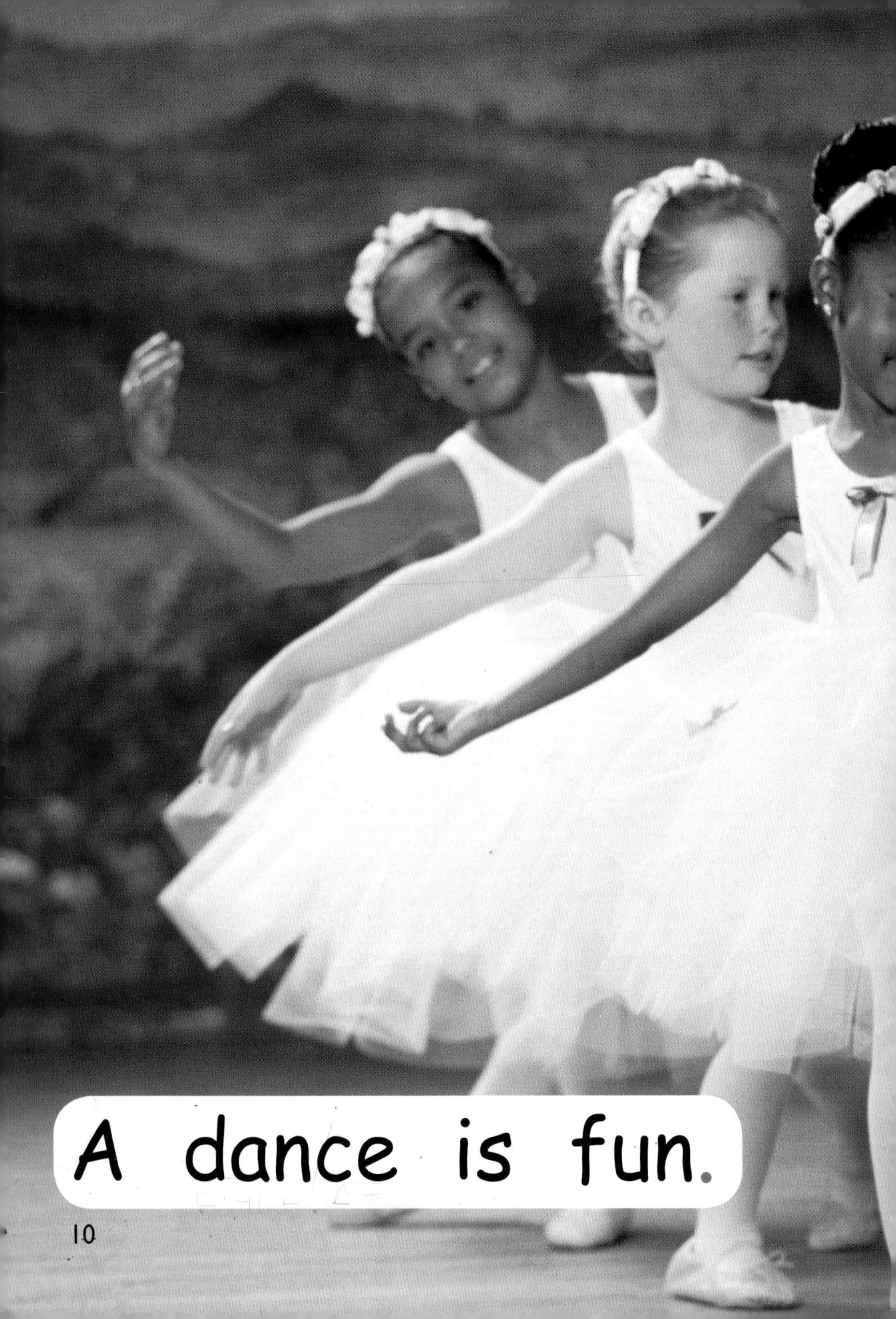

A dance is fun.

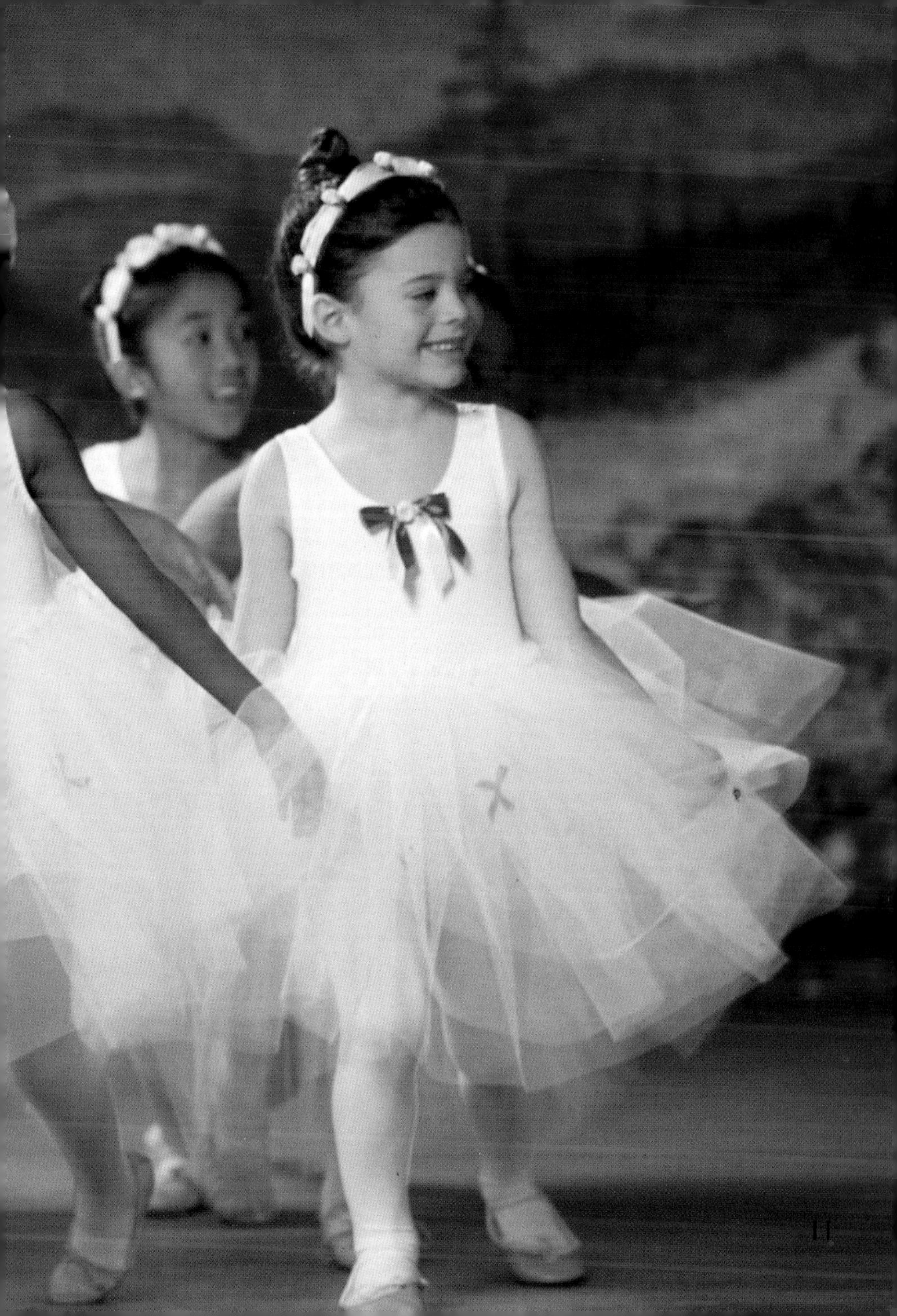

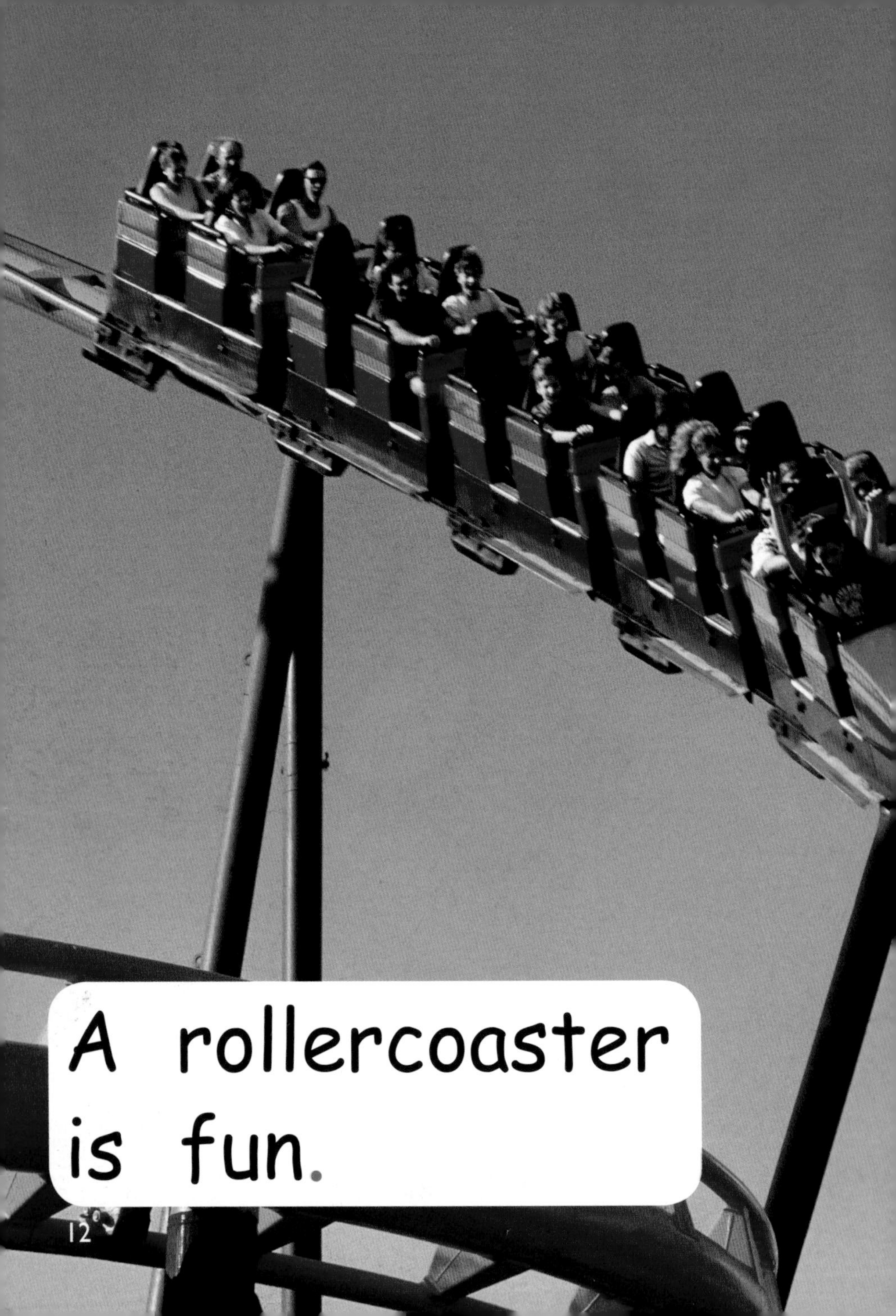

A rollercoaster is fun.

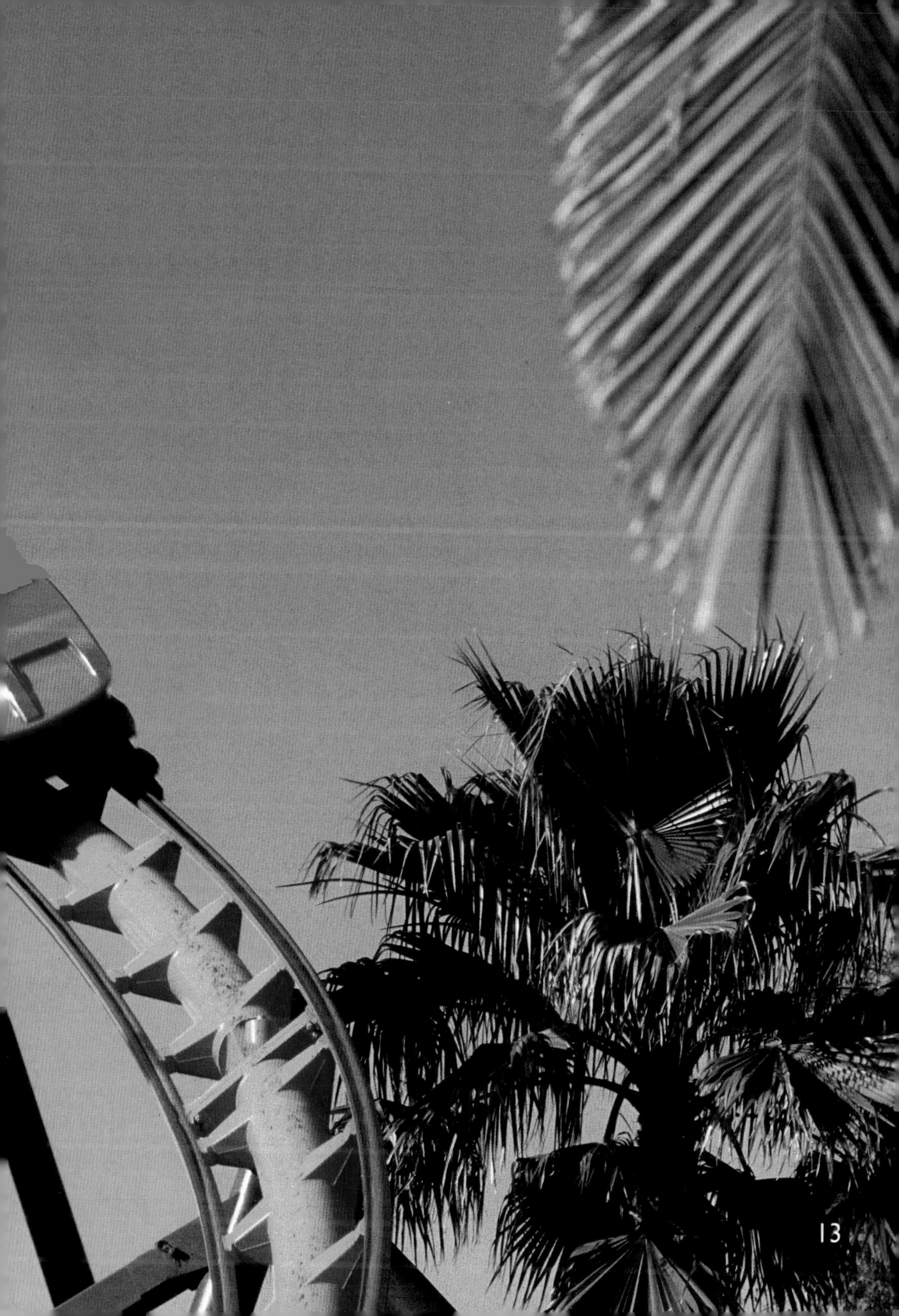

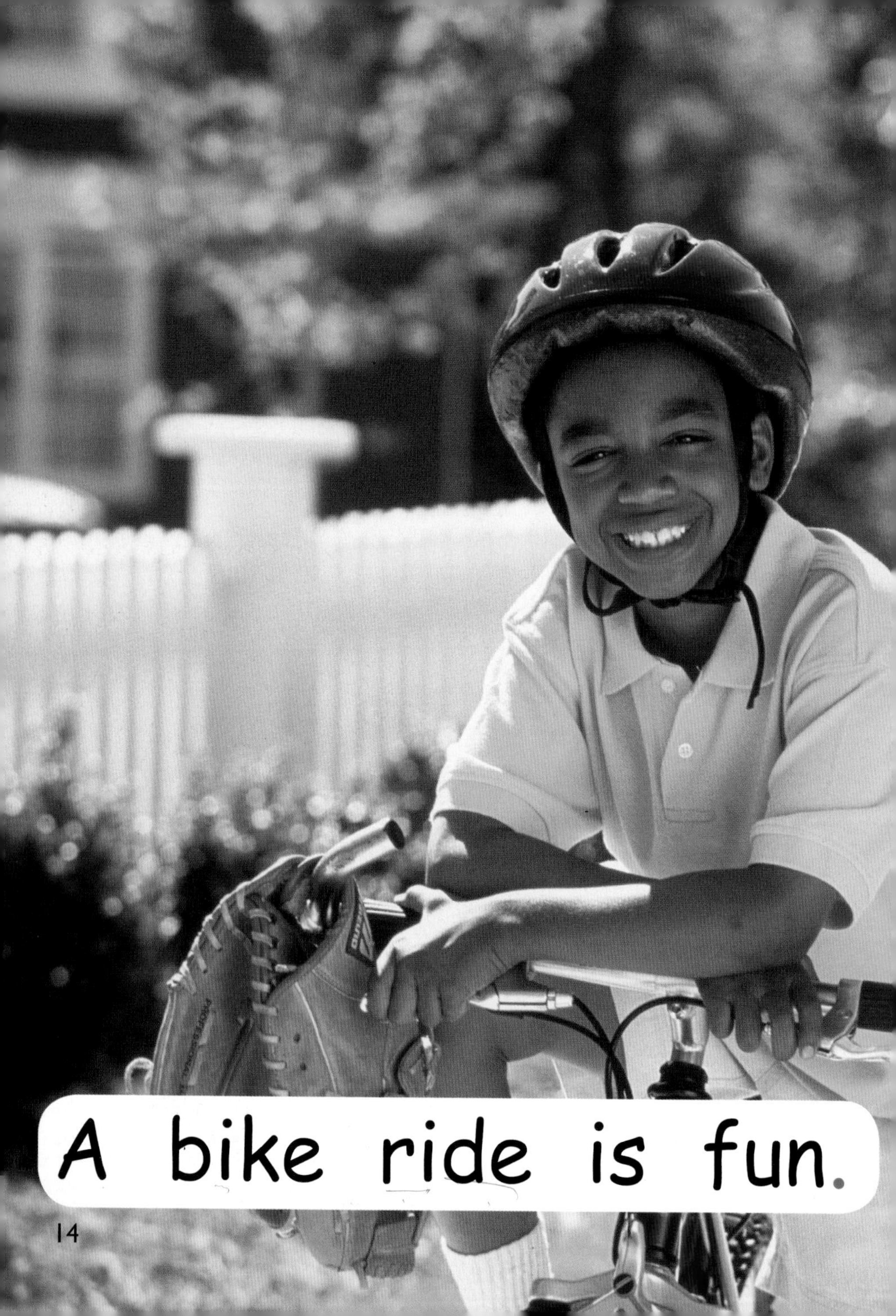

A bike ride is fun.

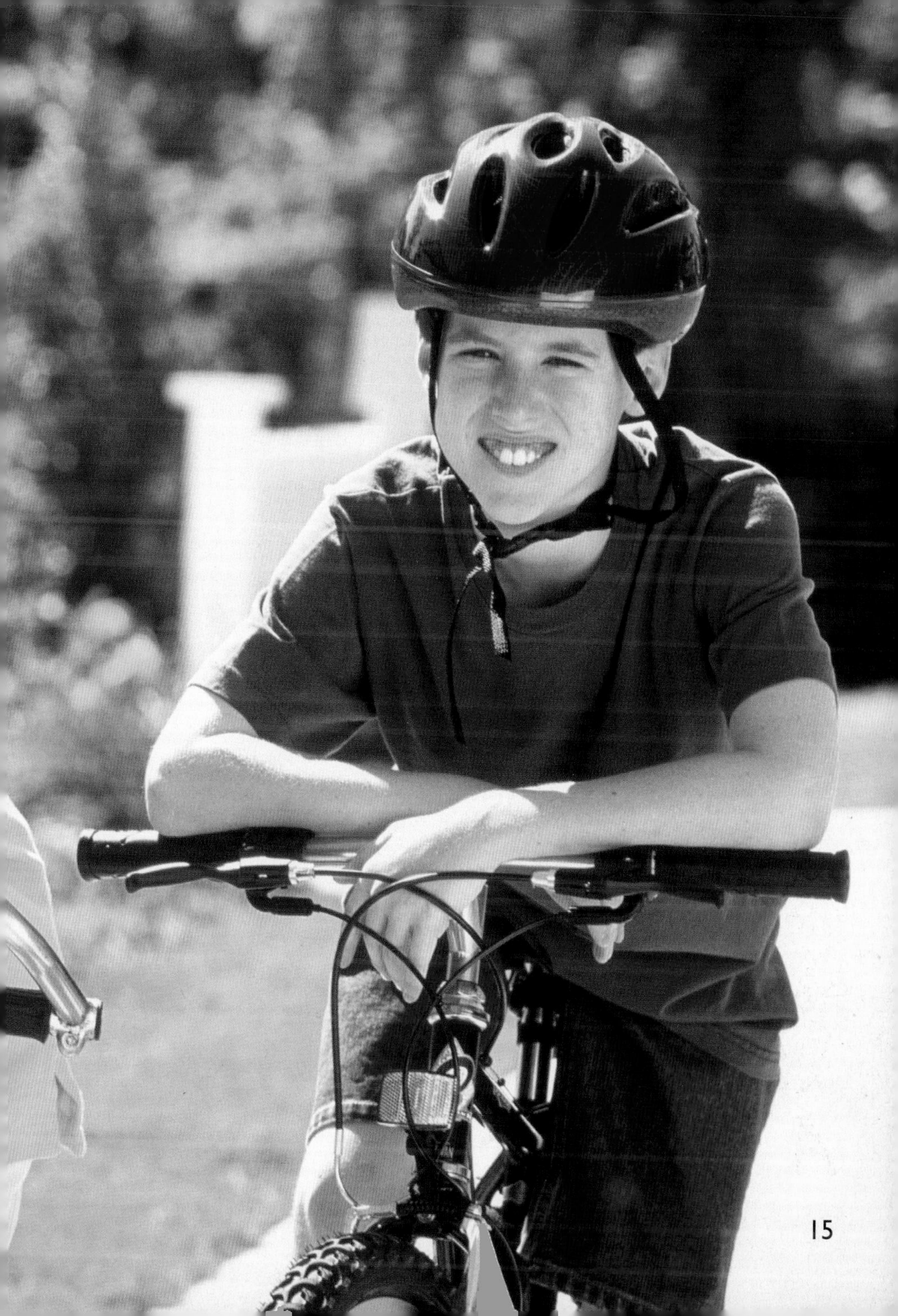

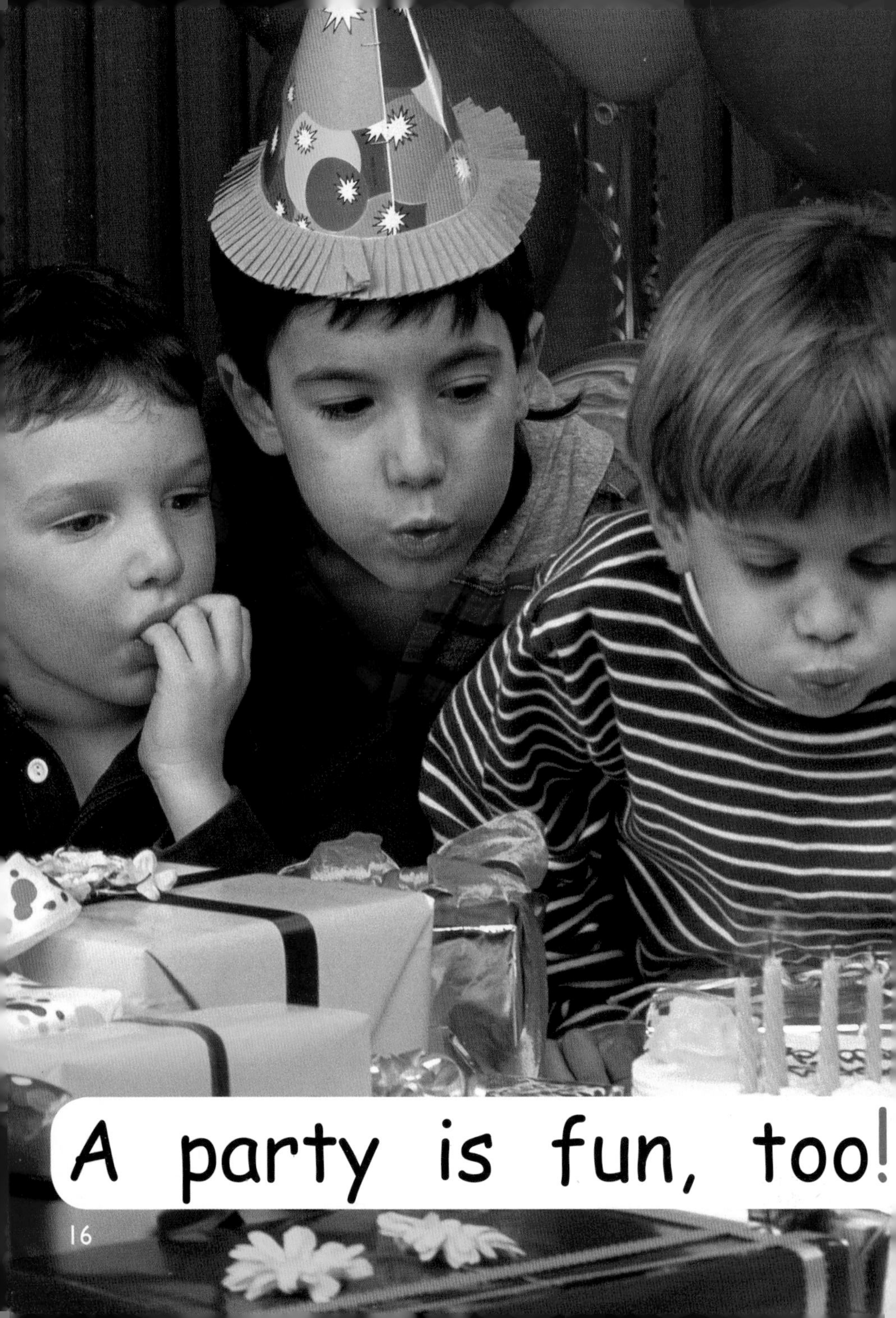

A party is fun, too!